£2.25
21st Sept '01

FANTASTIC WORLD

WATER LIFE

FANTASTIC WORLD

WATER
LIFE

STEVE PARKER

Miles Kelly
PUBLISHING

First published in 2001 by Miles Kelly Publishing Ltd
(Originally published in hardback edition 2000)
Bardfield Centre
Great Bardfield
Essex CM7 4SL

24681097531

Copyright © 2000 Miles Kelly Publishing Ltd

www.mileskelly.net
email: info@mileskelly.net

ISBN 1-84236-069-8

Design Jo Brewer
Page Make-up Helen Weller
Production Dawn Jones
Research & Index Jane Parker

Art Director Clare Sleven
Editorial Director Paula Borton
Director Jim Miles

The publishers wish to thank Ted Smart
for the generous loan of his illustrations.

Printed in China

Contents

World of waterlife

▶ Within the pages of this book all the animals shown in the main picture are listed in this panel. They are named in alphabetical order.

6

Walrus
All (or most) of the animals pictured in this book have their own entries, giving important details about their lifestyles, where they live, what they eat and how they breed.

Life began in the sea. Most of it stays there. From jellyfish to shellfish to swordfish, the oceans swarm with a vast array of creatures. This book shows water animals which are vertebrates (with backbones), mainly fish but also many reptiles like crocodiles and turtles, and mammals such as dolphins and seals.

Sea water is a 'soup' of tiny floating plants and animals called the plankton. These are food for smaller fish such as herrings and sardines. In turn the smaller fish are eaten by larger ones such as fearsome barracudas and ferocious sharks, building up the ocean food chains.

Fresh waters of rivers and lakes are also home to a huge variety of fish, from pygmy gobies to

You will always find a strange or amazing fact in this panel!

giant arapaimas in Amazon swamps. A few fish can move from salty water to fresh, by complicated tricks of body chemistry. Leaping salmons and wriggling eels attempt these perilous journeys.

Some air-breathing animals are water-dwellers. They include the biggest creatures on our planet, great whales. Others are peaceful plant-munching manatees, secretive and almost blind river dolphins, and long-tusked walruses and narwhals. All of these fascinating water creatures and many more are featured in this book.

Gills, lungs and fins

Lungfish look like links with the distant past, when prehistoric fish first crawled from the water, developed fins into limbs, gulped air and began to live on land as amphibians. Lungfish belong to a very ancient fish group which has been around for more than 300 million years. But they have continued to change or evolve through time and are now well adapted to life in slow muddy rivers, weedy lakes and shallow swamps. Like other fish, they can breathe oxygen dissolved in the water using their gills. But if the water lacks oxygen, for example when it is very shallow and warm, lungfish can also swallow air into their tube-like lungs.

African lungfish

This eel-like fish grows to 2 m long and is a fearsome hunter of smaller water creatures such as fish, frogs, crayfish, lizards and water birds. At breeding time the male wriggles and digs a hole in the sand or mud for the female to lay her eggs. He guards these while they develop and hatch.

Australian lungfish

The Australian lungfish is from a different ancient fish group to the South American and African types. It has fins with strong, fleshy bases like the famous 'living fossil' fish called the coelacanth. Also its Y-shaped, two-lobed lung is higher in the body, above the main guts, compared to the other lungfish. And it cannot survive buried in the mud if its creek or pool dries out. But like its cousins, the Australian lungfish is a powerful predator of almost any small water animal. It reaches a length of 1.5 m. These lungfish live naturally in the Mary and Burnett Rivers of north-east Australia. They have also been taken to other waterways in the region, in case accidental pollution or some other problem threatens this unique fish.

WHEN LUNGFISH GO TO SLEEP

South American and African lungfish can survive drought, when their water dries up, by burrowing into the damp mud beneath. As the dry season arrives and the rivers and pools shrink, the lungfish noses and presses the mud aside to form a vase- or tube-shaped chamber. It curls up in here and then its skin makes a layer of mucus (slime). This goes hard to form a waterproof lining or cocoon for the chamber. If the water disappears completely the lungfish seals the top of its chamber with another lump of mucus. Here it can pass the dry season, its body processes working very slowly, almost like a mammal in hibernation. This method of survival in the hot, dry season is called aestivation.

South American lungfish

Like other lungfish, the South American type does not breathe air through its nostrils as in land animals. It gulps air down its throat and gullet (oesophagus) and through a slit into its lungs. This lungfish reaches about 1.2 m in length and, like its African relative, its lower fins are long feelers.

In its cocoon in the mud, a lungfish can survive for several years. It does not eat, but gets its nutrients and energy by breaking down its own muscles.

- Bowfin
  (grindle or Great
  Lakes dog-fish)
- Longnose gar
  (long-nosed gar-
  pike or garfish)
- Spotted gar
  (spotted gar-pike
  or garfish)

The vast majority of fish belong to one enormous group, the bony fish. They have skeletons made of bone, not cartilage like sharks and rays. But among the 20,000-plus kinds of bony fish are several small groups which resemble their prehistoric cousins, almost like 'living fossils'. One is the bowfin group. It's so small that it has only one member – the bowfin. This fascinating fish lives in pools and streams in north-east and central North America. Fossils of its ancient cousins dating back to dinosaur times have been found across Europe and Asia. Gars were also once widespread. Now only seven kinds (species) survive in North and Central America.

Longnose gar
The longnose gar (shown opposite eating a threadfin shad) is a lurking predator like the other gars. It grows to about 1.7 m in length and lives in lakes and rivers throughout North America. Gars tend to wait among water plants, or alongside roots or branches, and dash out with a rush to grab their prey.

Spotted gar
The spotted gar has ideal camouflage for hiding among plants or bits of sunken wood. A gar's long mouth has many sharp teeth and the slender jaws can be flicked sideways at speed through the water to snap up victims. The anal (underside) fins and dorsal (back) fins are placed to the rear, near the tail, for bursts of speed.

Bowfin
This unique fish has many unusual features. It is named after its long back or dorsal fin which has a curve like a longbow. It also has a rounded rather than forked tail, and an almost rod-like shape with a blunt head and deep, wide body. It grows to about 100 cm in length. Bowfins are fearsome hunters of smaller fish, crayfish, freshwater shrimps, frogs and similar prey.

The male bowfin is usually slightly smaller than the female and he has a dark spot edged with yellow or orange at the base of his tail. He makes a shallow bowl-like nest on the bottom by biting away plants and swishing away mud and stones with his tail. After the female lays her eggs there he guards them fiercely. He also continues to defend the babies when they hatch.

FISH OUT OF WATER
Bowfins and gars have swim bladders which can work like lungs to breathe air, as in the lungfish (see page 8). This allows the fish to survive out of water for a day or more. Breathing air is a useful feature for fish that dwell in warm, still, stagnant water, often found in tropical marshes and swamps. This water has very little oxygen dissolved in it. So the fish obtains extra supplies by gulping air.

Another strange feature of the gars is their scales. These are diamond-shaped, thick and slab-like. They are called ganoid scales and give good protection, like armour. But they are much heavier than normal fish scales. They also limit movement because the body can bend or flex less when swimming.

**The male bowfin is the most dedicated father of all fish.
He protects his young until they grow to about 10 cm long.**

Bowfins and gars

Fish of the stagnant swamps

▶ Arapaima
   (pirarucu)
▶ Aruana (arowana)

The bony-tongue fish are exactly as their name suggests. The tongue in the floor of the mouth is strengthened by hard, plate-like pieces of bone. When the fish bites it does not so much bring its two jaws together, as press its tongue up against the roof of its mouth. Both the tongue and mouth roof have tooth-like projections and these crush and grind the prey – mainly other fish. Bony-tongues hunt in tropical lakes, rivers and swamps. They are mostly large and powerful fish, able to burst at speed from a weedy hiding place to ambush prey. The best-known member of the group is the arapaima – one of the biggest freshwater fish in the world.

Arapaima

The arapaima is known by various local names in its swampy home of tropical South America. It can 'breathe' in the normal fish way using its gills and also by gulping air down its throat into its swim bladder. The swim bladder's blood-rich lining then works like a lung to absorb the oxygen from the air into the body. This is very useful since warm, still, stagnant swamp water is very low in oxygen.

Tales were told of arapaimas swallowing full-grown people. This is very unlikely but the arapaima is still enormous for a freshwater fish. Its vast mouth can swallow a 50-cm prey whole. At breeding time the arapaima scoops a nesting hollow in the sandy swamp bed and guards its eggs there. It also guards the babies when they hatch.

Aruana

The aruana has a very distinctive shape, its flat-topped head making a straight line with its back and almost running into its tail. The fish grows to about 100 cm long and inhabits lakes and slow-flowing rivers in warmer parts of South America. The fleshy 'tentacles' on its upturned mouth are barbels. These are very sensitive to touch. They can also feel water currents and detect or taste certain substances in the water. Like the arapaima, the aruana has a long dorsal (back) fin and a similar anal (underside) fin, both set near the rear of its body just in front of the tail. When the fish swishes its rear body powerfully these fins help the tail to thrust it forward very quickly, usually to dash at prey.

MONSTER FISH FROM THE STEAMY JUNGLE

Many tales came from the remote swamps of the Amazon region about giant fish. Some were said to be so huge that they could swallow a person, an anaconda (the world's bulkiest snake) or a caiman (South American crocodile) in one gulp – or even a whole canoe! However it is difficult to judge the length of a fish half-hidden in muddy water. Also the size of the fish probably grew each time the story was told. The arapaima can swallow large prey but it feeds mainly on smaller food including shellfish and worms. Several other freshwater fish probably grow as large, including the massive catfish of rivers such as the Mekong in Southeast Asia.

There are sightings of giant arapaimas growing to more than 5 m in length and 200 kg in weight. But 3 m and 100 kg are probably more realistic.

Bony-tongue fish

A-maze-ing air-breathers

▸ Climbing perch
▸ Fighting-fish (Siamese or Thai fighting-fish, blue and red varieties)
▸ Three-spot gourami

The fish called anabantoids include many types familiar from the tropical aquarium – gouramis, combtails, paradise fish, climbing perches and fighting-fish. They are also called labyrinth fish because of the way they breathe. Normally they use their gills like other fish. But often the warm, still water of their tropical swamps and pools is low in oxygen. So the fish gulps air into two special chambers, one on either side of the head behind the eye. Each chamber has flaps that form a maze or labyrinth with a blood-rich lining. The air is trapped and its oxygen passes into the blood.

Climbing perch

About 25 cm long, the climbing perch lives in India, Southeast and East Asia. It makes good use of its air-absorbing labyrinth organs when it crawls from the water and wriggles across land, even over tree trunks and rocks. The perch usually does this to look for new water because its pool has almost dried up. It moves on land using its strong lower front fins (pectorals) and also the spikes on its gill covers, assisted by pushing with its tail. It can travel several hundred metres, usually at night when the air is cooler and damper, and there are fewer predators.

Fighting-fish

These small fish, only 5–7 cm long, live naturally in ponds and sluggish rivers in the Thailand region. The males vary from green to brown while the females are lighter olive-brown. However they have been bred for thousands of years to produce many varieties of fighting-fish, in different colours and sizes. Some have very long fins which they spread out as a threat to the rival.

Three-spot gourami

Wild gouramis live mainly in Southeast and East Asia, some reaching about 60 cm long. But many types have been selected and bred by people to produce a wide range of aquarium fish. These include thick-lipped, kissing, dwarf, lace, honey, sparkling and croaking gouramis. They are usually peaceful but at breeding times the males may attack other fish.

WHY FIGHTING-FISH FIGHT

Fighting-fish do not fight for fun or because they dislike each other. It is a natural instinct of many male animals at breeding time to show that they are strong and fit, and so a suitable mate for the female. Also fish may contest a living area or territory, where they feed and which they also need to possess in order to attract a mate. In the wild most such 'fights' normally involve body postures and displays rather than actual physical battle. However even in the wild the male fighting-fish is quite aggressive. It lifts its gill covers, stretches out its fins and may actually attack other male rivals. People have made these instincts stronger by selecting the most agressive males for breeding.

Fighting-fish can become so aroused that they even attack their own reflections on the inside of the aquarium's mirror-like glass side.

Labyrinth fish

The biggest family of fish

- Bigmouth buffalo
- Dace (dart)
- Goldfish
- Minnow
- Nase (sneep)
- Shorthead redhorse
- Stone loach
- Pike (northern pike)

The carp family is the largest of all fish groups with some 2000 different species. They live in fresh water and are mostly strong, deep-bodied and eat small food items such as bits of plants and water-living grubs. Different kinds of carp live mainly in the northern parts of the world. They have been taken to many other regions as food fish and for anglers. The common carp is now found almost worldwide and is an especially powerful and wily fish. In addition goldfish, koi, mirror carp, golden carp, leather carp and many other varieties have been bred as ornamental fish for ponds and lakes.

Dace
A quick and darting fish, the dace rarely grows longer than 25 cm. It likes clean fairly fast rivers and eats flies, grubs and other small animals.

Minnow
Many small or young fish are 'minnows' but the minnow is also a distinct kind or species. It is only 10 cm long and a common victim of bigger fish.

Nase
A fish of fast and gravel-bottomed rivers, the nase lives in Europe and Western Asia. It scrapes small plants off the stones with its hard, horny lips.

Pike
The pike is not a member of the carp group – but it does eat carp. It is a powerful predator up to 100 cm long with a mouthful of sharp teeth. It dashes out of water plants to ambush its prey.

Bigmouth buffalo
This massive, deep-bodied fish reaches 100 cm in length and lives in large lakes and rivers in eastern North America. It feeds on water plants and animals such as pond snails.

Goldfish
Wild goldfish live in weedy ponds and lakes across Central and Eastern Asia. They grow to 30 cm and have been bred in hundreds of colours, sizes and varieties for the aquarium.

Shorthead redhorse
Redhorses are types of sucker carp, named from their big, fleshy lips. They feed mainly on water insects, worms and grubs.

Stone loach
This small loach, only 15 cm long, lies camouflaged on the river or lake bed by day. It grubs among the stones for small worms, shellfish and similar food.

During the spring breeding season a female bigmouth buffalo lays up to half a million eggs.

Carp and their cousins

Silvery spotted leapers

‣ Atlantic salmon
‣ Dipper
  (a river bird)
‣ Leech
‣ Northern grayling
‣ River lamprey
  (brook lamprey)
‣ Trout (sea trout)
‣ Steelhead trout

Leaping waterfalls and rapids, on the way up their home river to breed, salmon are among the world's best-known fish. (And the tastiest.) Along with trout, pike, charr and smelt, they make up the large salmon family with more than 500 different species. Most live in northern parts of the world and are predators, hunting smaller animals for food. Many, like salmon and sea trout, are also migratory. They grow up in a river for a few years, journey out to sea for several more years, then return to the same river to spawn (lay eggs). They probably find their way by 'smelling' the exact mixture of chemical substances in their home stream.

Atlantic salmon
Salmon spend from 2 to 6 years in their home river, then head out to sea where they grow up to 1.5 m long, powerful and fast as they feed on smaller fish. After between 1 and 4 years at sea they head back upriver to breed in the gravelly stream where they hatched. Most then die but some make the journey twice.

Trout
Few fish are as widespread as the trout, which has been taken to all continents for angling and as food. The variety called the brown trout stays in a lake or river all its life. The sea trout (shown opposite) is more silvery and has a life cycle like the salmon, heading out to sea and then returning to breed.

River lamprey
Lampreys are not members of the salmon family but very strange fish with an almost prehistoric body design. They lack jaws. The mouth is a round sucker edged with tiny teeth. The lamprey usually lives as a parasite. It sticks onto a larger fish, its host, and rasps its way through the skin to suck its blood and body fluids.

Northern grayling
The grayling looks like a small trout, about 45 cm long, but with a larger sail-shaped back or dorsal fin. Like most members of the salmon family it has little, sharp teeth. Grayling live in Northern Europe and Northwest Asia and feed on small water creatures such as worms and insects.

Steelhead trout
Steelheads show the typical feature of the salmon family – the small lobe-like adipose fin on the upper rear body, between the main dorsal fin and the tail. The fish's blue-grey head looks like polished metal. The steelhead trout shown opposite is about to tackle a large leech on the stony river bed.

A salmon loses up to half its body weight as it battles its way against the current to the stream where it grew up.

Salmon and trout

Hard-shelled slow-movers

- Alligator snapping turtle
- Painted terrapin (pond turtle or painted turtle)
- Spike-shelled turtle
- Spiny softshell (spiny terrapin)
- Spotted turtle

Turtles and terrapins are far from fast. But they are well protected from harm inside their hard body shells. These mainly water-dwelling creatures, along with the land-living tortoises, are members of the reptile group called chelonians. There are about 180 different kinds of turtles and terrapins living in rivers, lakes, swamps and other freshwater habitats, mostly in northern and tropical regions of the world. Many eat a mixture of plant parts, especially soft leaves and stems of water weeds, and small animals such as worms, pond snails, shellfish, baby fish and young frogs. Female turtles lay eggs on land, in sand or mud or hidden under stones and logs.

Painted terrapin
Yellow stripes along the head and neck, reddish lines on the legs and bright markings around the 14-cm-long shell identify this common North American turtle. However its patterns are very varied, especially on the bright yellow underside. It eats mainly long, trailing water plants and also water grubs.

Spotted turtle
Most turtles are not active hunters. They lie in wait for passing victims or chomp leisurely on plants. Their dull colours and mottled patterns, like the spotted turtle's dotted patches of yellow, orange or red, help to camouflage them among the shady weeds and stones at the bottom of a lake or river.

Spike-shelled turtle
Young, newly-hatched turtles have softer shells than the adults. They are at risk from many predators such as herons, fish-eagles, mink and large fish. The spikes around the edge of this turtle's shell gradually lengthen and harden over the first two years for excellent protection.

Spiny softshell
With a shell up to 45 cm long, the spiny softshell is a powerful predator of fish, crayfish, water insects and even small water birds. Its name comes from the small, spiky lumps on the front of the shell above the neck. This turtle lives in quiet ponds and creeks in eastern, central and south-eastern North America.

Alligator snapping turtle
This is the largest freshwater turtle in North America, growing to more than 75 cm long and 90 kg in weight. It lies on the bottom of a muddy lake or slow river, its ridged shell camouflaged by weedy growths to look like a jumble of stones. The turtle holds its mouth wide open to reveal a small, narrow, pale, fleshy flap on the floor of its mouth. This wriggles like a worm and attracts fish, crayfish and similar animals. If they come to check the 'bait' the turtle snaps shut its massive, sharp-edged jaws and swallows the victim whole – or slices it in half. As an alternative, the turtle can lunge upwards and grab passing prey in the sharp, hooked front parts of its jaws. The female alligator snapper lays 20–40 eggs in early summer.

Snapping turtles feed on carrion such as drowned deer and pigs, finding them by smell. They have been used to locate the bodies of people murdered and thrown into deep lakes.

Freshwater turtles

The widest, toothiest grin

Crocodiles have been lurking in rivers and swamps since the time of the dinosaurs, more than 150 million years ago. The crocodilian group has 22 members including 14 species of crocs and seven types of alligators and caimans mainly from Central and South America. The final member is the curious gharial from the Indian region with its very long, slim, tooth-studded snout. It catches fish by a sideways sweep of its jaws.

22

Gharial
This is one of the most aquatic crocs, rarely leaving the water except to breed. It has more than 100 small, pointed teeth for grasping slippery fish prey.

Nile crocodile
The Nile croc lives in many watery areas of Africa. It grabs large animals or birds which come to drink, drags them under the surface to drown, then tears off chunks to swallow.

American alligator
Once rare in the wild, this alligator has recovered its numbers and lives across the south-east USA. The mother 'gator' builds a nest mound of old plants and lays her eggs inside. The plants rot and release heat which incubates the eggs for about nine weeks. Like many croc mothers she guards the eggs and watches over the babies for several months.

Black caiman
Caimans are similar to alligators and live mainly in South America. Largest is the black caiman of the Amazon region at 4.5 m long. It was hunted so much for its meat and leathery skin that it is now excessively rare.

The largest living reptile is the saltwater crocodile, also called the Indo-Pacific, Australian or estuarine crocodile. It grows to more than 7 m in length.

Shy, secretive and sightless

- Amazon river dolphin (bouto or boutu)
- Ganges river dolphin (Ganges susu or side-swimming dolphin)
- Indus river dolphin (Indus susu)

Most dolphins live in the open sea. Their secretive and little-known relatives are the river dolphins from some of the largest rivers in the world. There are five kinds or species – two in the Indian region, two in South America and one in China. River dolphins have tiny eyes and are almost blind, because sight is little use in their muddy water. However they can swim fast and accurately using the squeaks and clicks of echolocation or sonar, like other dolphins (and also bats). They find their prey of fish and similar animals by sound too, grabbing the victims in their long beaks equipped with more than 100 small, sharp teeth.

Amazon river dolphin

This freshwater dolphin lives in the Amazon, Orinoco and connected large rivers in South America. Although most river dolphins are quite shy, the Amazon dolphin is inquisitive and sometimes approaches a small boat, or even comes near a swimmer if she or he keeps still and quiet. These dolphins often move around in small, close-knit groups. They are very agile and frequently swim on their sides or even upside down. Amazon river dolphins from the Amazon itself tend to be lighter pink in colour and larger, about 2.3 m long and 120 kg in weight, compared to those from the Orinoco. Another dolphin, the tucuxi, also swims in the fresh waters of the Amazon but it is greyer and much smaller, only about 1.4 m in length.

Ganges river dolphin

This is one of the largest river dolphins, reaching a length of 2.4–2.6 m. It is a powerful swimmer and often leaps straight up like a missile bursting out of the water. The alternative name of 'susu' comes from the sound these dolphins make when they breathe out through their nostrils – the blowhole on the forehead. They eat many types of fish including carp and catfish, as well and shrimps.

Indus river dolphin

The Indus dolphin is very similar to the Ganges dolphin at about 90 kg weight. It is hunted for its body oil which is used in some local medicines. Like other river dolphins, its search for food has been severely affected by dams built for hydro-electricity and to water farm crops. All river dolphins are rare and affected by overfishing, pollution, drowning in nets and traps, and noisy boats which interfere with their delicate sonar systems.

The Indus river dolphin and the whitefin river dolphin of the Chiang Jiang (Yangtze) in China are two of the world's rarest mammals. Each numbers just a few hundred.

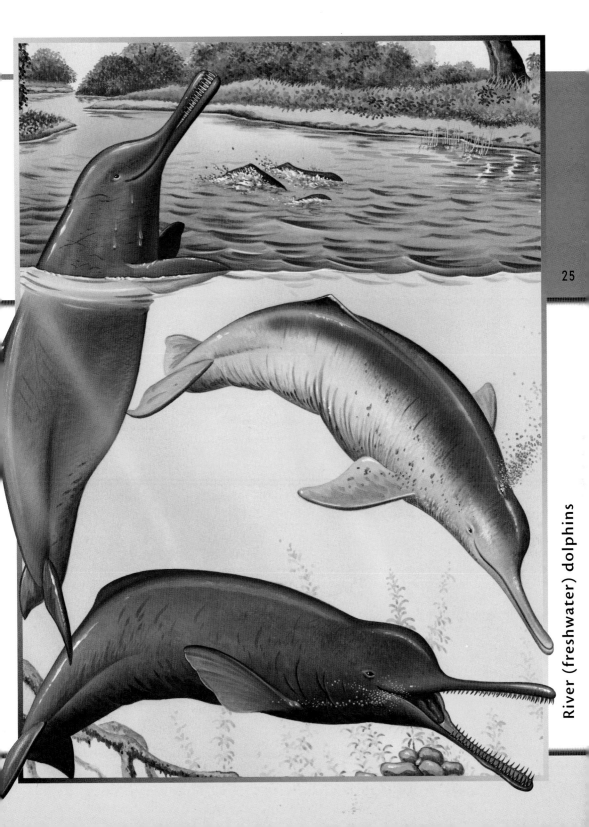

River (freshwater) dolphins

Wings underwater

Rays and skates are flat-bodied cousins of sharks, with skeletons made of cartilage (gristle) rather than bone. Rays may look like flatfish such as plaice but they are quite different. A flatfish rests and swims on its side while a ray rests on its true belly or underside. However both types of fish are flat for the same reason – living on the sea bed. Rays swim by rippling or flapping their 'wings' which are very large, fleshy pectoral fins. There are about 320 members of the ray group including mantas, skates, sawfish and guitarfish. Nearly all are predators. They eat mainly shellfish, crabs, worms and similar animals which they grub up from sea-bed mud.

26

Blue stingray
Stingrays can indeed sting, using the sharp spine part of the way along the thin tail. The venom (poison) is extremely painful, even deadly. The blue stingray grows to 1.5 m long. It is especially dangerous since it likes shallow water and hides in the sand of holiday beaches around the Indian and Pacific Oceans.

Atlantic manta
Unlike most rays, which spend hours lying camouflaged on the ocean bottom, mantas spend much of their time swimming near the surface. The Atlantic manta is a sizeable fish but smaller than its huge Pacific relative. The name 'manta' comes from the dark colour and shape of the fish, which is like a cloak or mantle. The alternative name of devil ray comes from the two fleshy flaps on the head, which look like horns. The flaps scoop water into the mouth as the manta swims by powerfully beating its vast 'wings'. As the water passes through the mouth, small creatures of the plankton are filtered out by comb-like parts on the gills. The manta may also swallow the occasional larger fish, squid, shrimp or prawn.

Spotted eagle ray
Eagle rays have especially large wing-like pectoral fins. Seen from the front they resemble the eagles of the air as they swoop gracefully at speed above the sea bed. As in several kinds of rays, the female's eggs hatch and grow inside her body and she gives birth to fully-formed young.

Common skate
This skate is a massive, powerful fish some 2.7 m long, almost 2 m wide and more than 110 kg in weight. It preys on all kinds of victims at all levels in the water – not only smaller surface fish like herrings but also other rays, small sharks like the dogfish, and also flatfish, crabs and lobsters on the sea bed.

Atlantic guitarfish
Guitarfish look like a mixture of ray and shark with longer, slimmer bodies than most other rays. The Atlantic guitarfish is found in warmer waters along the east coast of North America. It reaches about 70 cm in length and crunches up crabs and shellfish with its large, flat crushing teeth.

The Pacific manta is the largest ray with a length of about 5 m and a 'wingspan' of almost 7 m.

Rays and skates

The most feared fish in the sea

The word 'shark' brings an image of the supreme predator – a sleek, fast, powerful hunting fish, with a wide mouth full of razor-sharp teeth, and incredible senses able to detect faint traces of blood in the water from 5 km away. This is true for many sharks such as the blue, mako, tiger and the dreaded great white. However the biggest sharks of all, the whale and basking sharks, are peaceful plankton-feeders and almost harmless. All 360 or so different kinds of sharks have skeletons made of cartilage (gristle), like rays, rather than made of bone as in other fish.

28

Great white shark

At some 6 m in length, the great white is the largest predatory shark. It swims in warmer waters around the world. It is not actually white but grey or brown on top.

Whale shark

The world's largest fish, the whale shark takes in huge mouthfuls of water and its specialized gills filter out small floating animals and plants.

Blue shark

The super-streamlined blue lives in warm seas and is 3.7 m in length. It has very long side fins and eats surface fish like herring and mackerel.

Starry smooth-hound

Hound sharks and their smaller cousins, dogfish, are named from their habit of prowling in small shoals or 'packs' for bottom-living prey like crabs, prawns, worms and shellfish. This shark grows to 1.5 m.

Basking shark

Almost as large as the whale shark, at about 11 m long and 3–5 tonnes in weight, this giant fish is named because it often lazes in the sunlit surface waters. Like the whale shark it filters plankton from the water using comb-like bristles or rakers on its gills. It sometimes gathers in large shoals.

Sandbar shark

Light brown to match the sandy bottom, this shark is a shallow-water predator in tropical and subtropical regions. It is a fast swimmer but sometimes lies still on the sea bed, only its gill muscles working so it can obtain oxygen from the water.

The whale shark grows to a length of 17 m or more and a weight of about 10 tonnes.

Snakes of the sea

- Conger
  (conger eel)
- European eel
  (common eel)
- Green moray
  (green moray eel)
- Pink snake eel

Eels look like snakes but they are really fish with long, wriggly bodies. There are more than 600 kinds (species) and they live all over the world, mainly in warmer seas and oceans. Three of the normal fish fins – the dorsal (back), caudal (tail) and anal (underside) – join to form one long flap that wraps around the body. There are also the usual two pectoral fins on the front sides of the body, as in other fish. Eels are mostly lurking, sharp-toothed predators. They can wiggle their long, thin bodies to hide in cracks in the rocks, among coral or in holes in the sea bed. They catch mainly smaller animals such as fish, prawns, shrimps, sea-snails and worms.

Conger
Divers who mend harbour walls or explore sunken shipwrecks are always wary of the conger. It hides away, camouflaged by its dull grey-blue colour, with just its head poking out. It peers through the water with its large eyes, ready to seize any passing prey in its strong jaws. This eel can grow to almost 3 m long and easily fit a human hand into its mouth. Like most eels it travels into deep water to breed, producing small, leaf-shaped larvae or young (as explained below). These gradually change shape as they grow.

European eel
One of the world's most common fish, this eel lives almost everywhere in Europe, North Africa and East Asia, including coasts, rivers, lakes and ditches. Females grow to about 100 cm long but males are barely half this size. These eels eat almost anything and survive out of water for several hours. They even wriggle across fields to reach new, land-locked reservoirs and canals. European eels swim to the West Atlantic to breed. The small, leaf-shaped, see-through young drift back over 3–4 years with the ocean currents.

Pink snake eel
There are more than 200 kinds of snake eels. They live mainly in shallow tropical oceans and some have bright colours. But many kinds, such as the pink snake eel, are more like worms than snakes. They have very long and bendy bodies, and leathery skin which lacks scales. They dig burrows by wriggling tail-first into the mud or sand on the ocean bottom. Then each snake eel hides in its tunnel with just the front of its head sticking out, to watch and smell the water for victims.

Green moray
Divers' tales about moray eels say that their bites are poisonous, and once they have closed their teeth on something they never let go. Certainly morays are very fierce and always ready to snap, rather than slither away like most other eels. But some tales are not entirely true. A moray soon lets go if it is hauled above the water. And the bite is not poisonous, although it may go septic (bad) from germs on the moray's teeth. The green moray grows to about 2 m in length and hides among seaweed and eel-grass.

Moray eels are named after a nobleman of Ancient Rome, Lucinius Muraena. To show his power and wealth he kept these eels in tanks – more than 6000 of them!

Flying fins and needle noses

Why do flyingfish fly? They don't – at least, not true flapping flight. They swim fast just under the water's surface, then leap above to glide on their large outstretched fins. This is usually to avoid predators such as tuna and dolphinfish which are chasing them just below. Flyingfish belong to a large group of more than 800 kinds of fish which also includes toothcarps, silversides, killifish, needlefish and halfbeaks like the ballyhoo. Halfbeaks are named after the oddly shortened upper jaw. Needlefish such as the garfish have very long, thin, sharp jaws. All of these fish are active predators, chasing and eating smaller sea creatures.

Garfish
The garfish is quite different from the gars or gar-pikes of North America. It is found in the North Atlantic Ocean and the Mediterranean and Black Seas, where it speeds through the surface waters after prey. Garfish grow to about 90 cm long and can skitter just above the surface by swishing their tails hard.

Flyingfish
Slightly smaller than the Atlantic flyingfish, at about 30 cm in length, this type has only two enlarged fins. It cannot glide quite so far or with such skilled control. Flyingfish in a shoal which are threatened by a pack of larger predators sometimes leap from the water in their hundreds, like a flock of silvery, scaly birds.

Ballyhoo
The ballyhoo lives mainly in the West Atlantic, in shallow water where it eats small creatures as well as bits of plants such as sea-grass. Its strange mouth may help it scoop food from the surface. Like garfish, the ballyhoo and other halfbeaks can skim or skitter across the surface, with the front part of the body in the air.

Houndfish
The largest type of needlefish, almost 1.5 m long, swims fast and flicks its head sideways in a flash to seize a fish in its long, sharp-toothed jaws. Then, almost like a heron or similar bird, it tosses the fish around to swallow it head-first. Houndfish skimming the surface have flipped into small boats and given severe bites!

Atlantic flyingfish
The very large pectoral fins work like wings so the flyingfish can glide for many seconds through the air. The Atlantic flyingfish also has slightly enlarged pelvic fins, behind and below the main ones, for better control. It reaches a take-off speed of about 50 km/h and can stay airborne by thrashing its tail to and fro 50 times each second, with the longer, lower part just dipped into the water. Back under the water the flyingfish folds up its large fins like fans and holds them against the sides of its body so they do not slow it down. This flyingfish reaches 40 cm in length and lives in shoals. Sometimes a stormy gust of wind lifts several of them so high during their glides that they land on the deck of a ship.

A good glide for a flyingfish covers about 100 m in 10 seconds, cruising at an average height of 1.5 m above the surface.

33

Flyingfish and garfish

In the warm midwater gloom

The gloomy midwater zone covers depths of about 100 m to 1000 m, depending on the clarity of the sea water – below this it's nearly or completely pitch black. In the tropical and subtropical oceans many little-known, large-eyed, colourful fish swim in the dimness, often sporting long or spiky fins. The types shown here belong to the tongue-twisting zeiform, lampridiform and beryciform groups. More simply they are all predators, hunting mainly smaller fish, prawns, shrimps, squid and other victims. Some, like the John Dory and the lantern-eye, spread into shallow waters. Others range into colder regions, like the dealfish off Iceland.

34

Dealfish

No other fish has such an unusual fan-like tail, pointing upwards as though joined to the body at right angles compared to other fish. There is also a distinctive red fin along almost the entire back. Dealfish grow to 2.5 m in length and dwell in the eastern North Atlantic. They feed on small squid and fish.

Oarfish

At 7 m from its snout to the end of the tapering tail, the eel-like oarfish is one of the longest of all fish. However it is far from bulky, being shaped like a strap or ribbon and only 10 cm wide. The tall crest is formed by the first few spines of the dorsal fin, which runs virtually the length of the body.

John Dory

Valued as a food fish, the John Dory has a tall but thin body when seen head-on. Like the other fish shown here it is equipped with a protrusible mouth which opens forward like a wide tube to engulf victims. The John Dory is 65 cm long and found in the Mediterranean Sea and eastern Atlantic Ocean.

Long-jawed squirrelfish

The 60-cm-long squirrelfish has large eyes, not to see in the faint light of midwater, but to hunt on shallow reefs at night. It inhabits rocky inshore areas of the western Atlantic and Gulf of Mexico. The vicious rear-pointing spine on the gill cover at each side of the head helps to deter enemies.

Lantern-eye

Most fish with light-producing organs live in deep water. But the lantern-eye, 30 cm long, favours shallows around Southeast Asia. The fish is named from the curved patch below each eye. This appears white by day. However at night it glows lantern-bright and even flashes on and off when the fish is agitated.

Opah

This bright, bulky animal, also known as the moonfish, is found in midwaters around the world. Strong and heavy, up to 1.5 m long and 75 kg in weight, it lacks teeth and looks far from speedy or agile. Yet the opah still manages to catch fast-swimming prey such as squid and whiting in its protruding, thick-lipped mouth.

At about 7 m, the oarfish is the longest bony fish. (Some sharks are longer but they have skeletons of cartilage or gristle, not bone.)

Spiny-finned fish

A tough life at the seaside

Almost any rock pool has its small fish – mainly gobies with their slippery leathery skin, big blunt heads, strong spiny fins and tapering tails. The shore is a very tough habitat with crashing waves, rolling boulders, hot sun, driving rain, chilly winds and the rise and fall of the tides. Gobies are hardy little fish and there are more than 400 kinds around the world, living mostly along shores and in shallow seas, with some in lakes and rivers. They tend to stay on or near the bottom, using their large fins to grip seaweed and rocks. Dragonets are also shore-dwelling, bottom-living fish. Like gobies they are in the huge group called perch-like or spiny-finned fish.

Pallid goby

The pale, mottled silvery-brown of this goby is ideal camouflage on a sandy sea bed scattered with rocks and stones. Its fin spines are stiff and sharp, especially along the back (dorsal) fins. This puts off gulls, otters, bass, octopuses and other predators. The pallid is average length for a goby, about 12 cm.

Neon goby

Gobies of tropical waters tend to have brighter colours than those in colder seas, to be noticed among the corals. The neon goby often rests on its pectoral (front side) fins, as though leaning on its 'elbows'. Like most gobies it only swims in short bursts. Otherwise it remains still, watching for food or danger.

Tiger goby

Like other gobies, the tiger goby feeds on a variety of small or young water creatures such as sand shrimps, prawns, crabs and sea-snails. Its stripes conceal it among the fronds of seaweeds and sea-grasses such as eel-grass. Its thick-skinned, tough-scaled, slimy body allows it to wriggle between pebbles.

Spotted dragonet

Dragonets spend most of their time lying on or half-in the sea bed, or grubbing in sand, mud and pebbles for small animals to eat. Their eyes and gill openings are high on the head. The spotted dragonet is 15 cm long and the male has taller fins and brighter colours than the female.

Common dragonet

The male dragonet (shown opposite) is 30 cm long and a very colourful fish, with two tall back fins like brightly patterned yacht sails. The female is smaller and mainly brown, with shorter fins. Common dragonets live along the shores of the East Atlantic Ocean and Mediterranean Sea.

Greater sand-eel

Sand-eels are not proper eels but long, slim, eel-shaped members of the perch group, and close cousins of gobies. They grow to about 20 cm long and can quickly wriggle like worms into the sandy sea bed, almost out of sight. Sand-eels are common food for larger fish and birds such as puffins.

The world's smallest fish is a goby. The Philippines dwarf goby lives in a few lakes and streams on a few Philippine islands. It is this big: »≈›

Shore and rock pool fish

Dangerous or just curious?

- Barbu
- Blue bobo
- Great barracuda (picuda or becuna)
- Southern sennet (Southern barracuda)
- Striped mullet

If all 'big fish' stories were true, barracudas would be as dangerous as those other greatly feared fish, sharks. But this applies only to one of the 18 kinds of barracudas – the great barracuda. It is a big, fierce hunting fish with long, sharp teeth. There are records of it following and even biting divers. However some tales of its savage attacks may be larger than life. Barracudas belong to the vast group of perch-like or spiny-finned fish. So do mullets. Most fish are either saltwater or freshwater. But mullets are unusual. They can swim from the salty sea into the brackish (part-salty) water of estuaries, where fresh water from a river flows into the ocean.

Barbu
The barbu is a member of the fish group known as threadfins or tasselfins. The front spine-like parts or rays of the pectoral fins, at the front sides of the body, are long and thin like lengths of string. They are sensitive and used for feeling, both by touching objects and by detecting ripples and currents.

Great barracuda
The great barracuda is well known as a fish with great curiosity. It swims near divers and follows them, watching their movements and actions. This quiet menace is one reason for the barracuda's fearsome reputation. Some attacks may be the result of barracudas being provoked or surprised by divers or swimmers. But there are also tales of sudden bites for no apparent reason. Another strange feature is that barracudas may be very aggressive in one area, yet shy and peaceful in another. They live in most warmer waters but are often met in the Caribbean and West Atlantic Ocean. They form shoals around shores and reefs when young. The large adults dwell alone, mainly in deeper waters.

Blue bobo
The bobo is a mainly bottom-dwelling type of threadfin. It lives in the warmer southern waters of the Indian and Pacific Oceans and grows to 60–80 cm long. It noses in the mud for food with its 'overhung' snout, the upper jaw being longer and more protruding than the lower jaw (as in the anchovies).

Striped mullet
The striped mullet reaches 90 cm in length and lives in warmer coastal regions around the world as well as out in the open ocean. It feeds by sucking mud and sand into its mouth and filtering out tiny edible bits using its specialized gills. The bits are swallowed and ground up in its muscular stomach-like gizzard.

Southern sennet
There are several types of smaller barracudas or sennets living in the Indian, Pacific and Atlantic Oceans – mainly in the warmer waters to the south. Some grow to about 1.6 m in length. They are powerful, sleek, sharp-toothed predators and live similar lifestyles to the great barracuda.

Great barracudas probably grow to about 2 m long, although some people claim they reach much larger sizes.

Barracudas and mullets

Fish with big appetites

Since prehistoric times people have caught and eaten tunas and mackerels. These fast-swimming members of the vast perch-like (spiny-finned) fish group are close relatives of marlins and swordfish. To swim so fast, more than 50 km/h, tunas have huge muscles along the body and a slim, curved tail. The muscles make up more than two-thirds of the fish's whole weight, which is why tunas are such valuable food fish. A tuna also has a spiny front dorsal (upper back) fin, a softer rear dorsal fin, and small finlets along its back to the tail.

40

Bluefin tuna
This massive fish can grow to more than 4 m in length and 700 kg in weight. It lives in all seas and oceans but moves around in shoals with the seasons. Sometimes bluefins stay near the surface, chasing fish such as herring and mackerel. Sometimes they stay in deep water and use their big eyes to hunt squid.

Skipjack
A small tuna about 100 cm long, the skipjack is found in great numbers in the Pacific Ocean, where shoals can be as large as 40,000. Vast curtain-like nets are hung in the sea to catch these tunas. However the nets trap seabirds, seals, porpoises, dolphins and similar air-breathing animals – which soon drown.

HOT-BLOODED FISH
Fish are cold-blooded, with a body temperature the same as the water around them – except for tunas. Their muscles are so large and so active that they produce lots of heat, which keeps the tuna 'warm' in the cold sea. Warm muscles work even better, which is why tunas can swim so far so fast.

Atlantic mackerel
Mackerels are smaller relations of tunas. Atlantic mackerels are only 40 cm long. However they swim in vast shoals and have been caught for centuries as food fish. Like their huge relatives they are fast-moving, hungry predators. However during winter they lie still near the sea bed and hardly eat.

King mackerel
This strong, fierce predator has sharp, blade-shaped teeth and may prey on its smaller mackerel namesakes. The pattern along its sides varies from one fish to another and is probably for camouflage in the shadowy water. This pattern may form mainly stripes or be more broken up into spots or marble-like swirls.

Spanish mackerel
These mackerels live mainly in the central region of the Atlantic Ocean, especially in the waters off Europe and North Africa. They are larger than common mackerel at about 4–5 kg in weight. The finlets in front of the tail, as in other mackerels and tunas, help with speedy swimming.

The largest king mackerels grow to 1.5 m long and about 45 kg in weight.
This is 100 times the weight of the common or Atlantic mackerel.

Swords, sails and speed

Swordfish, sailfish and marlins are all billfish – some of the most spectacular and exciting fish in the ocean. They are named after their long, pointed snouts or bills ('beaks'). They are big, powerful, extra-streamlined predators of smaller fish, squid, seabirds and other ocean creatures. These fish have the tails typical of the fastest swimmers. The tail is thin and stiff, shaped into a slim curve or crescent, with a narrow stock or base where it joins the body. The fish does not swim by long, snake-like waves of the body. Instead its whole body shakes or vibrates to wave the tail from side to side, many times each second, in a rapid frenzy of surging power.

Wahoo
The wahoo is not a billfish but it is a close relative. Like billfish and its even closer cousins, the tunas, it belongs to the huge group called perch-like or spiny-finned fish. Wahoos reach about 2 m in length and are found in all tropical seas. They can get up speed faster than any other fish, from 0 to 70 km/h in 2 seconds.

Sailfish
Probably the world's fastest fish, the sailfish has a long, tall dorsal (back) fin. At top speed it folds this and its other fins against the body to improve streamlining. At breeding time the female sailfish releases more than 5 million tiny eggs into the water. Only a few survive and grow to adult size, 3.5 m, in 6–7 years.

Blue marlin
Like other billfish the huge blue marlin lives and hunts mainly in the upper surface waters. These marlins regularly reach 3.5 m in length and weigh 200 kg, and a few grow even larger, over 500 kg. Marlins are much prized by anglers because of their strength, stamina and amazing leaps from the water.

White marlin
Most billfish like the white marlin make seasonal migrations. They move north or south in summer and return to the tropics in winter. The white is the smallest of the four kinds of marlin, weighing about 70–80 kg. It lives in the warmer regions of the Atlantic Ocean. (Largest is the black marlin at 700-plus kg.)

Swordfish
The swordfish may weigh 650 kg and be almost 5 m long. But about one-quarter of this is its 'sword' formed by the long upper jaw. Like other billfish it catches prey by speed and power. But how? It's very unlikely that the swordfish stabs them. More probably it swims at speed through a shoal of smaller fish, waving its head from side to side to slash through the water at the prey. The bill may actually hit victims. But it also creates powerful ripples or shock waves in the water which stun and daze them. The swordfish then returns quickly and swallows its meal. The sword grows gradually – young swordfish have much shorter noses in proportion to their bodies. One swordfish drove its nose 55 cm into the timbers of a wooden ship.

Measuring the top speed of big, fast ocean fish is very difficult. But the sailfish can probably reach speeds of about 100 km/h.

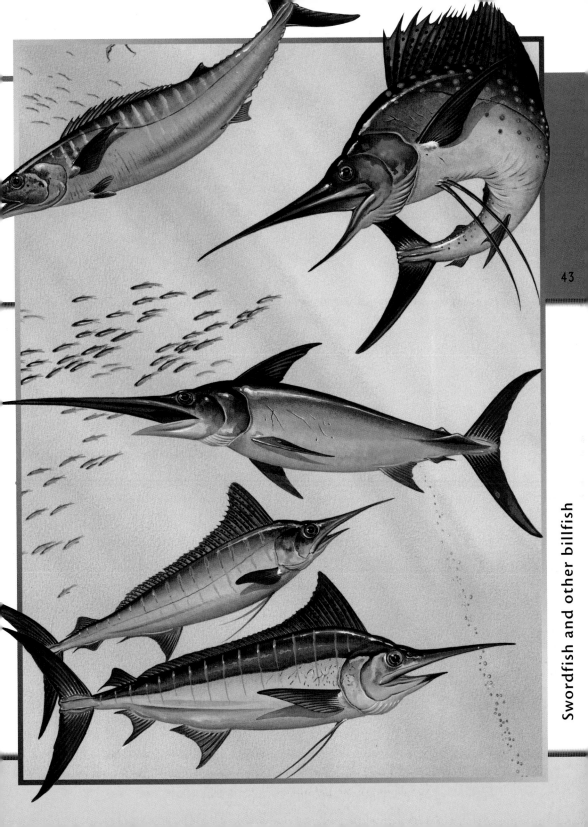

Swordfish and other billfish

Fish in their millions

Few fish have affected world history as much as the herring. This smallish, silvery ocean swimmer has been caught in such huge numbers that it has made cities and countries rich. People have even gone to war over who should fish the vast shoals that swim in the North Atlantic. Close relatives of the herring are sardines (pilchards) and anchovies. These are also food fish of global importance. There are about 290 different kinds (species) in the herring group and most live in massive shoals in the open ocean. They feed by filtering tiny animals and plants of the plankton, using long, comb-like parts called rakers on their gills to sieve the water.

44

Pacific sardine
Each large area of ocean around the world has its own type of sardine. Most are about 20–30 cm long. Like herring, they filter tiny planktonic food and live in gigantic schools which are caught by giant fishing boats. They move with the seasons, away from the tropics for summer and back to warmer waters for winter.

Atlantic menhaden
The menhaden, about 45 cm in length, is another herring relation that swims in great shoals. Huge quantities are caught but they are not usually eaten by people since their flesh is very oily. Instead these fish are used to make fertilizers, fish oils and nutrients added to farm animal feeds.

Atlantic herring
The herring grows to 40 cm long and is pale silver. It is found in shoals several kilometres long with hundreds of thousands of fish. At least it was. So many have been caught by fishing boats that they are now less numerous. Herring are a main link in ocean food chains. They eat tiny plants and animals in the plankton, and they are food for larger fish like marlin and tuna, as well as seabirds, seals, dolphins and many other ocean hunters.

Alewife
The alewife, a type of herring cousin called a shad, migrates like the salmon. It grows up along the Atlantic coasts of North America, then swims up rivers to spawn (lay eggs). It reaches about 40 cm in length. However some alewives stay all their lives in fresh water, mainly in the Great Lakes, and are smaller.

Gizzard shad
This fish is named after its large gizzard – a muscular bag like the stomach which grinds up its food. Gizzard shads are 50 cm in length and have a very long rear spine or ray on the back (dorsal) fin. Unlike other shads, they stay in the sea to breed and do not swim up rivers.

One of the largest herrings is the wolf herring. It grows to 3.5 m in length and has long, sharp teeth as big as a real wolf's fangs – a truly fearsome fish.

Herrings and sardines

Hard-shelled swimmers

Large tropical rivers like the Amazon are sometimes visited by a very specialized group of reptiles – marine turtles. These slow, heavy creatures can hardly move on land. The females haul themselves ashore every two or three years to lay their eggs, usually burying them in beach sand. Then they return to the water, where they spend most of their lives wandering in search of food. The youngsters hatch in two to three months, dig themselves up to the surface and scurry to the waves, avoiding predators like gulls, lizards and otters. In water the turtle swims elegantly with its large, flipper-like front legs. These flap rather than row, almost like flying underwater.

Loggerhead
The loggerhead is named after its large, bulky head which contains very powerful jaws. Turtles have no teeth but their jaws have very sharp, horny edges. The loggerhead can easily crunch up crabs, prawns, whelks, oysters and similar shellfish, as well as sponges and seaweeds. It grows to about 100 cm long.

Hawksbill turtle
The shell of this turtle has beautiful swirling patterns and was used as the original 'tortoiseshell'. Like other large turtles, the hawksbill is now protected by wildlife laws. It is named after its narrow, hooked mouth, which it pushes into rocky crevices for prey such as crabs and fish.

Green turtle
Seaweeds, and especially seagrasses, are the green turtle's main food. But, like other big turtles, if it is hungry it eats whatever may be available, including jellyfish and shrimp-like krill. Green turtles grow to about 1.2 m long and were once widely hunted for their shells, meat, eggs and to make 'turtle soup'.

Leatherback
The massive leatherback is the largest living turtle. Like other turtles and tortoises it has a two-part body casing. The hard domed part over its back is the carapace. The flatter part on the underside is the plastron. In a typical turtle these are made of flat slabs of bone covered with plates of a hard, horny substance. But the leatherback lacks the bony slabs and horny plates. Instead it has a casing of tough, leathery skin, almost like the rubber of a car tyre. Leatherbacks have weak mouths and feast mainly on jellyfish.

The leatherback turtle grows to 1.7 m long and weighs 600 kg.
And its huge front flippers can measure 2.6 m across.

Estuarine and marine turtles

Peaceful plant-eaters of the sea

Manatees and dugongs are called 'sea cows' because they peacefully munch seaweeds and other water plants – just as cows munch grass on land. In fact these large, tubby mammals are more like hippos with flippers and live in tropical waters. The dugong has a slightly forked tail, like a whale, and lives in the Indian Ocean from the east coast of Africa across to Western Australia. The three kinds of manatees all have rounded, spoon-like tails. The West African or Senegal manatee, similar to the American manatee shown here, is found in the rivers and lakes of West Africa. The Amazon or South American manatee is smaller and also a river-dweller.

American manatee

This type of manatee is found in warm waters from Florida, USA around the Caribbean to northern South America. It lives in the sea and also swims into rivers and lakes. It can grow slightly larger than the dugong, 4.5 m long and 1500 kg in weight. Like the dugong, the manatee's front limbs are flipper-shaped. It has no back limbs at all, but its tail has become flattened for swimming. Manatees eat huge amounts of water plants – and this can come in useful. In some areas they have been captured and moved to rivers, lakes or canals which are choked with weeds. The manatees steadily chew away the weeds and clear the waterway. However manatees, like dugongs, are at risk of injury by boats. And if they become stuck in underwater fishing nets they will drown.

Dugong

The dugong grows to about 4 m long and more than 800 kg in weight – far bigger than a cow on land! It prefers shallow, sheltered coastal waters. Its favourite food is seagrass which grows down to depths of about 5 m. A female dugong does not have her first baby until the age of about 20, and she feeds it on her milk (as all mother mammals do) for about two years. So, although she may live to 50 years old, she only produces five or six young. This slow breeding is one reason why dugongs, having been hunted for their meat, are now rare in some areas. Also in today's busy coastal waters both dugongs and manatees are at risk from ship and boat propellers, hulls, waterskis and jetskis.

THE LEGEND OF THE MERMAID

Dugongs and manatees are mammals and so they breathe air. They usually come to the surface every minute or two and take a breath, although they can stay under for several minutes in an emergency. They also poke their heads above the surface to look around for danger, mates, food and other items of interest. Old-time seafaring people said that the creature's large head with its beady eyes could almost be mistaken for a person in the water. The sudden appearance of a manatee or dugong head may have led to ancient sailors' tales of mermaids. In olden times sailors spent many lonely months on the ocean. Seeing a mermaid might be the result of wishful thinking!

The manatee has the longest guts (intestines) of any animal – more than 40 m!

Manatees and dugongs

Flipper-footed fish-eaters

- Leopard seal
- Northern elephant seal (male and female)
- Steller sea-lion (male, female and young)
- Walrus (male and female)

Seals, sea-lions and the walrus belong to a mammal group known as pinnipeds, which means 'flipper-feet'. They are slow and awkward on land but in water they swim with tremendous speed and grace. Sea-lions 'row' with their front flippers. On land they can prop themselves up on these flippers and waddle along. Seals are even better swimmers and use their rear flippers, but they can only wriggle or 'hump' on land. Most pinnipeds live along coasts and hunt fish, squid and similar prey.

Steller sea-lion
This is the largest type of sea-lion, the male growing to almost 3 m in length. It lives along the shores of the North Pacific Ocean and dives down nearly 200 m in search of squid, octopus and fish. As in many sea-lions and seals, the males come ashore at the start of the breeding season and fight each other to gain a patch of beach, called a territory. Males without territories have little chance of mating with females.

Leopard seal
With its leopard-like spots and wide, sharp-toothed mouth, this Southern Ocean seal is 3.5 m long. It's a fierce, fast hunter, but not of fish. It preys on penguins, seabirds – and other seals.

Walrus
Like many pinnipeds, the male walrus is much larger than the female. He grows to 3.3 m long and over 1200 kg in weight. A walrus uses its tusks to lever shellfish from sea-bed rocks. It also eats crabs, starfish, worms and other bottom-dwelling creatures. Walruses live all around the Arctic Ocean.

Northern elephant seal
The male elephant seal with his huge, floppy nose grows to a massive 5 m in length. Most of his weight, as in other pinnipeds, is a thick layer of fatty blubber under the skin. This keeps in body warmth when swimming in cold water. It also makes the body shape more streamlined for faster swimming.

Elephant seals show the greatest size difference between the sexes of almost any animal. Males weigh more than 2300 kg. Females are less than one-third this size.

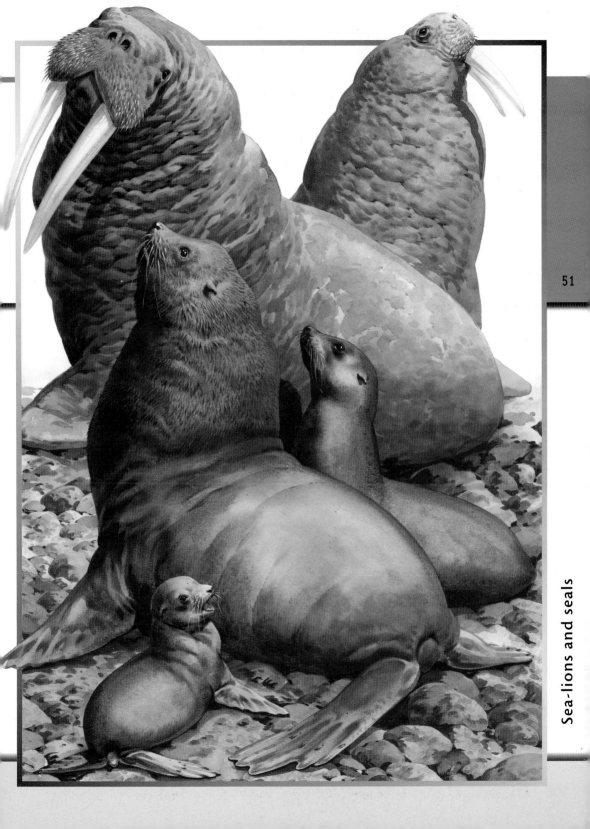

Grey shapes among the waves

Porpoises are smaller cousins of dolphins and whales. There are six kinds or species, ranging from 1.2 to about 2 m in length. They look like dark-grey, blunt-nosed dolphins. But, unlike dolphins, porpoises seldom jump out of the water. They are usually seen just breaking the surface of the sea to breathe through the blowhole (nostrils) on the top of the head. Most kinds live in small groups of up to five, often leaving one group to join another. Porpoises hunt fish and squid but also take other small animals such as prawns and krill. They find prey by eyesight and by sonar-type clicks, as in dolphins, and catch food with their small, spade-like teeth.

52

Common porpoise

This is the most common and also the most often-seen porpoise – partly because it has a very wide distribution, including the waters of the North Pacific and North Atlantic Oceans, and the Mediterranean and Black Seas. It is also because the common porpoise swims nearer shores and is not so shy of ships and busy waterways as the other species. However it is nowhere near as common as it once was, having suffered a drastic fall in numbers in the Baltic, North and Mediterranean Seas. This is probably due to pollution and lack of food (caught by fishing boats). It lives in groups of about 10 and feeds mainly on fish and cuttlefish.

Spectacled porpoise

This is one of the most attractive of the porpoises, named after the white eye markings which make it look as if it's wearing spectacles. It is also one of the largest porpoises. The males grow to an average length of 2 m, the females to about 1.8 m. Their range includes the coastal waters of South America, especially the eastern shores, also the Falkland Islands to the south-east and possibly across the ocean to New Zealand. Fish such as anchovies as well as squid probably feature in their diet.

Burmeister's porpoise

Unusual in being dark grey nearly all over, apart from a few light patches on the belly, Burmeister's is a rare and little-known type of porpoise. It is found mainly off the coasts of South America, from Peru around the southern tip of the continent and north to Uruguay. It has also been sighted around the Falkland Islands. It has a much flatter head than other porpoises and grows to about 1.6 m long and 50–60 kg in weight. Like other porpoises, Burmeister's probably eats mainly fish and squid.

The common porpoise has more than 100 teeth and
can dive to depths of 90 m.

Big smiles and clever tricks

Some people are lucky enough to meet real dolphins swimming free in the sea. These marvellous creatures, which are smaller cousins of whales, are warm-blooded mammals like us. But they have no fur, their arms are shaped like flippers, they have no legs either, and their tails have two broad side flukes. All 32 kinds of dolphin hunt fish, squid and similar sea animals. They take in air through their nostrils, which form the blowhole on top of the head, so they must surface every minute or two to breathe. Dolphins are fast and agile in the water. They naturally leap, somersault and spin for no obvious reason. Perhaps they are having fun?

Bottlenose dolphin

This is the type of dolphin usually seen at sea life centres. It lives in all warmer oceans and grows to about 3.5 m long. Dolphins are intelligent animals. They learn new tasks rapidly and in captivity they even invent their own tricks to play on their keepers.

Fraser's dolphin

This average-sized dolphin is about 2.3 m long and 85 kg in weight. All dolphins make clicks and squeals to find their way by echolocation and to keep in touch with their group.

Risso's dolphin

Risso's grows to 4 m long and weighs 370 kg. Its skin scars probably come from fights with its own kind at breeding time.

Spinner dolphin

This is one of the most acrobatic dolphins. It jumps high out of the water and spins around like a top. It lives in the open ocean and eats mainly fish.

Common dolphin

For centuries artists have painted and sculpted these dolphins, which have very variable markings and colours. They live worldwide.

Spotted dolphin

The speckles of this dolphin may help to camouflage it in dappled surface waters. However dolphins have few enemies, mainly large fish like sharks.

The smallest dolphin is probably Heaviside's dolphin of the waters around South Africa. It is about 1.2 m long and weighs only 40 kg. The largest dolphin is the killer whale.

Dolphins

Master hunters of the ocean

The killer whale is one of the world's supreme hunters. At 9 m in length and 3 tonnes in weight, it is far bigger than any land predator. It's also larger than the biggest flesh-eating shark, the great white. Killer whales are very intelligent. They live in family groups, or pods, and work together to surround prey such as shoals of fish. False killer whales are slightly smaller and do not have such a tall back fin or white patches on the sides of the body. But they too are fearsome hunters of many kinds of prey. Pilot whales grow to about 6 m long. Like the killer whales, they are not really true whales – they are very big members of the dolphin family.

Killer whale
The female killer whale is slightly smaller than the male, at about 6–7 m long. Also the fin on her back is shorter and more curved or crescent-shaped compared to the male's. His tall, pointed fin may be 2 m high – the largest back fin of any dolphin or whale. Killer whales live in all seas and oceans, even in cold Arctic and Antarctic regions. They feed on many kinds of fish, squid and similar prey. They are also the only type of dolphin or whale that regularly hunts warm-blooded victims including other dolphins, also porpoises, great whales, seals, sealions and seabirds such as penguins. Full-grown killer whales have no natural enemies and even in the wild they may survive to an age of 60 years or more. In captivity they are found to be intelligent.

False killer whale
Like the killer whale, the false killer makes a huge variety of sounds. Some are used to communicate with other members of its group. Other sounds work like sonar (sound radar) and bounce off objects. The false killer hears the echoes and so finds its way in dark or muddy water.

TOGETHER IN A POD
A typical killer whale pod has about 10 members. There is usually one large male, three or four adult females, and several youngsters who are both males and females. They may stay together for years. The babies tend to stay and grow up in the pod, generation after generation.

Long-finned pilot whale
Pilot whales are named because they often swim alongside ships and boats. They seem to guide the boat across the sea, in the way that the expert human sailor called a pilot guides ships into a port or through dangerous waters. Pilot whales tend to stay near the coast rather than head for open seas. They live in the North Atlantic and also in all southern oceans. Their main foods are fish and squid. These dolphins stay together in their pod for many years, in a group of six to ten. Sometimes several pods join together for a time to form a larger school. Like all whales and dolphins, pilot whales are mammals and breathe air. So they have to make frequent visits to the surface.

The killer whale is the fastest swimming mammal, powering along at speeds of 55 km/h.

Killer and pilot whales

Noisy whales of northern seas

▶ Beluga (belukha or white whale) (female and calf)
▶ Narwhal (tusked whale) (male)

58

The beluga and the narwhal make up a small group called white whales – although the narwhal is mottled cream, blue, grey or brown on its back and sides. They are both unusual among whales because they have no dorsal (back) fin, and they can bend their necks to look around and curl their lips into facial expressions. Also they live in very cold water among the icebergs and pack ice of the Arctic Ocean, especially along shores and estuaries and in shallower coastal waters. The beluga in particular is a very noisy whale. It makes a huge variety of squeaks, moos, clicks, chirrups and bell-like clangs that can even be heard above the water.

Narwhal

The narwhal has only two teeth. In the male one of these, the upper left incisor, keeps growing and becomes a long, sharp tusk with a twisted spiral pattern. It can reach nearly 3 m in length. The other tooth stays about 20 cm long. The whale's body may grow to more than 5 m long and weigh 1.5 tonnes. The female narwhal also has two teeth and one may grow into a tusk, but this is much shorter and may not even grow beyond her lips. A narwhal uses its lips and tongue for feeding, not its teeth.

Like belugas, narwhals live in small groups of adults and young. These often gather into larger herds of hundreds. The herds migrate along the coast with the seasons, to follow the shoals of fish and other food and to keep clear of the spreading winter ice.

Beluga

The beluga's many sounds and noises help it to keep in touch with other members of its group or herd. The sounds also bounce off nearby objects like rocks and animals and the beluga hears the echoes. Like a bat in air, this echolocation system helps the whale to find its way in dark or muddy water and to detect food. The beluga also 'makes faces' at other herd members by opening and twisting its mouth into a variety of smiles, frowns and grins. Belugas grow to 5–6 m in length and eat a wide range of food including fish, squid, worms, shellfish, shrimps and crabs. They feed mainly on the bottom of the sea and use their pursed lips to suck worms from the mud and shellfish out of their shells.

Beluga calf

A newborn baby beluga is 80–90 cm long. It is also brown in colour, which changes to slatey blue-grey by about one year old. Then it gradually lightens to pure white by its adult age of five years. The youngster feeds on its mother's milk for up to two years and hardly ever leaves her side during this time.

UNICORN OF THE SEA

The narwhal's long tusk looks like the head horn of the mythical horse known as the unicorn. Exactly why this whale has a tusk is not clear. Sometimes males come to the surface and use their tusks like swords to 'fence' each other. This may be to gain success in mating with females.

About one male narwhal in 50 has two tusks.
It looks like a combination of whale and walrus!

White whales

Giant hunters of the depths

- Dwarf sperm whale (Owen's dwarf sperm whale, rat-porpoise)
- Pygmy sperm whale (small, lesser or short-headed sperm whale)
- Sperm whale (cachalot, spermacet or spermaceti whale)
- Squid

Sperm whales spend much of their time in the blackness of the deep ocean, hunting their prey by the clicks and squeals of their sonar. They regularly dive more than 1000 m below the surface and stay under for an hour as they hunt near the ocean floor for fish, squid, crabs and similar food. The sperm whale's enormous head makes up one-third of its whole body length. It contains a waxy or oily substance known as spermaceti which was once used to make candles, cosmetics, creams and very high-quality lubricating oil. Sadly, hunting for this and for other body parts, like the flesh and blubber, has made sperm whales rare.

Sperm whale

The mighty sperm whale is more than 20 m long and 40 tonnes in weight, making it the largest toothed whale – and by far the largest predator or meat-eater on Earth. When whales surface to breathe they can be recognized by the pattern of moist, steamy air they snort out through their blowholes. In the sperm whale this 'blow' is angled forwards and to the left.

The massive bulging head of this whale is filled mainly by the spermaceti organ, which has layers of oily wax. These act as a kind of sound-lens to focus the whale's huge grunts of low-power sound which can stun its prey. The spermaceti organ also works as a buoyancy device. As the whale descends it becomes denser or heavier, making the whale less buoyant and so the dive is easier.

Dwarf sperm whale

Similar in shape to a porpoise, without the usual sperm whale's bulging forehead, the dwarf sperm whale reaches about 2.5 m in length. It is found most often in warmer seas, especially off the coasts of South Africa, India and Australia, and rarely in the open ocean like the pygmy sperm whale.

Pygmy sperm whale

Pygmy sperm whales grow to about 3.4 m long and 500 kg (half a tonne) in weight. They have a varied diet including shrimps, crabs, fish, octopus and cuttlefish as well as plenty of the usual squid. They catch their food at depths of about 100 m, in coastal waters and far out at sea.

BATTLE OF THE TITANS

Sperm whales sometimes plunge down 2000 m or more for two hours or longer. After returning to the surface for a couple of minutes to breathe they descend again into the depths. Sometimes a group of sperm whales dive together and work as a team to round up their prey. Like dolphins, they find food by sonar or echolocation, making squeaks, clicks and grunts that bounce off nearby objects. A sperm whale has up to 50 cone-shaped teeth in its slender lower jaw but no teeth showing in the upper jaw. Its skin is scarred by marks from the suckers and the hard, horny, beak-like mouth of its deadly enemy. This is also its biggest prey, with a 6-m body and 10-m tentacles – the giant squid.

Ambergris was once used to make the delicate scents of very expensive perfumes. Which is odd because this substance comes from inside the guts of sperm whales!

Sperm whales

The bottom of the sea

The world's biggest habitat is also its most mysterious. The ocean depths are endlessly black and cold. Fish and other animals live on the 'rain' of rotting debris floating down from above – or eat each other.

62

Gulper eel
Prey is scarce in the vast blackness of the deep ocean, so fish like the gulper have large mouths to grab whatever they can. This eel is a relative giant of the depths at 60 cm long.

Snaggletooth
Several deep-sea fish have rows of glowing or bioluminescent spots along their sides. These may signal to others of their kind at mating time.

Tassel-chinned anglerfish
Hardly larger than your thumb, this anglerfish has extraordinary fleshy tassels on its chin that resemble seaweed.

Tripod fish
The tripod fish 'walks' along the soft mud of the sea bed on the long spines of its two lower side fins (pelvics) and lower tail. It probably eats small shrimps and similar shellfish.

Long-rod anglerfish
The body of this anglerfish is only 15 cm long but its bendy, whip-like 'fishing rod' can be more than 20 cm in length.

Dragonfish
Like snaggletooths, dragonfish are predators of smaller creatures. They rise nearer the surface at night to follow their prey such as very young squid.

Sloane's viperfish
The first spine or ray on the back (dorsal) fin of the viperfish is very long and flexible. It has a blob-like tip that glows in the darkness. Small creatures come to investigate and the viperfish grabs them in its wide, gaping jaws lined with long, needle-shaped teeth. The viperfish looks fearsome and is one of the larger predators of the ocean depths. Yet it is only 30 cm long. The general lack of food in the deep sea means animals are mostly small.

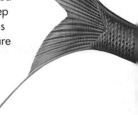

The tripod fish is one of the deepest dwelling of all fish, found more than 6000 m below the surface.

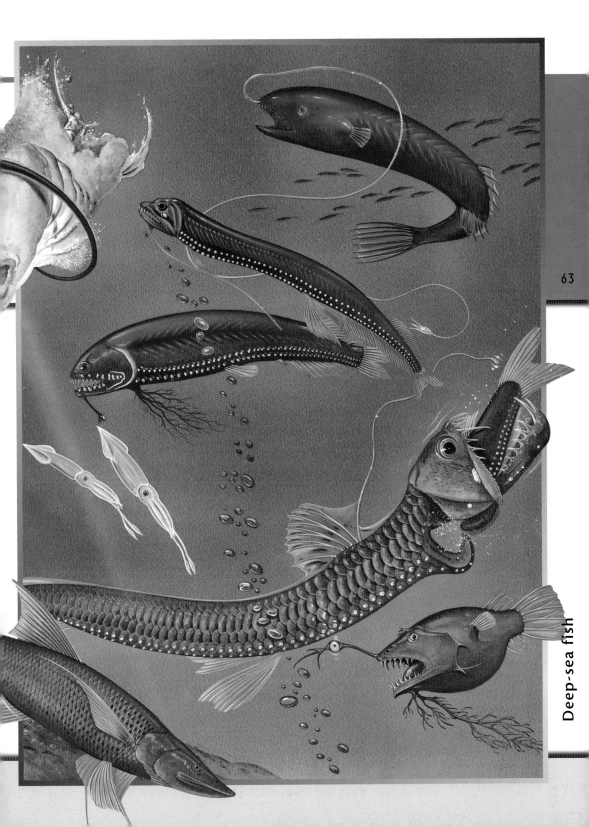

Deep-sea fish

Index